the day barque

A REVIEW OF POETRY, PROSE AND THE ARTS

Apollo Poetry Society

The Day Barque

A review of poetry, prose and the arts

Volume 3, Number 1 – August 2015

The Day Barque

A review of poetry, prose and the arts

Published by Apollo Poetry Society
P. O. Box 716, Oregon House, CA 95962

Volume 3, Number 1
Cover: *Swan* by Genya Gritchen
Editors: Judith Grace, Stefano Petrizzo
Design and Production: Margaret Jean Campbell

Visit www. thedaybarque.com

This book is set in Adobe Caslon Type Text.

Printed in the United States of America

Volume 1, Number 1: December 2013
Volume 2, Number 1: July 2014
Volume 2, Number 2: December 2014
Volume 3, Number 1: August 2015

ISBN-13: 978-0692484814 (Apollo Poetry Society)

ISBN-10: 0692484817

1. Poetry 2. Art 3. Literature 4. Spirituality

Volume 3, Number 1

August 2015

Contents

ARTISTS

Apollo Poetry Society

Joep Jilesen

Love Affair with a Doe

Without thinking I hit the brake
On this warm Sunday afternoon.
She's halfway across the road
Before her head turns to me.
She stops and circles around on high heels.
Where I came from is safer ground—
She must think.
I open the side window and
Look into her round brown eyes.
She stares back at me.
Her ears move and turn,
Then open up in my direction.
Slowly she walks back
To the side of the road.
Shyly she nibbles on a little bush.
She looks at me again,
Less shy this time.
I look at her beautiful bearing.
Quickly I check the rearview mirror
Before my eyes swing back to her.
With three big jumps she crosses the road.
I watch until the trees cover her from sight.

Joep Jilesen

Hummingbird Sharply Turns

As I feel the swoosh of its wings on my neck
Time fast forwards and backwards in an instant,
Leaving a dent in my sprawling mind.
I do not hear it stop.

A mountain of worries has a melting snowcap.
Its beauty revealed in colorful flowers every spring.
Reflections in the lake form two pyramids,
Creating a diamond in crystal blue water.

One breath cannot describe the road downhill.
My legs feel the long grass cutting fresh wounds in them.
I can see clearer now: we are the only two left.
Your green eyes mirrored in my sunglasses.

No comparison can be made to the days of our marriage.
We are a waterfall of shadows pouring out of our mouths.

Joep Jilesen

An Angel on Each Shoulder

We had planned this months ago.
Two boys and four girls,
Ardennes by bike.
No gears, no experience with hills.

We used a self-drawn map from an atlas.
Saddle bags, rain jackets on the back carrier.
Tents and tire repair kit, of course.
Food to carry us through the first two days.

Blame it on the signposts.
We got lost in a foreign country.
We ate our last can of fish that night,
Divided by six.

We arrived the third evening
With storm clouds pouring rain
On what once were roads
By the Semois river.

The soaked meadow became a battlefield
Where the tents would never get dry again.
What did we care?
We had an angel on each shoulder.

Beauty of the World — Linda Carter Holman

Joep Jilesen

Harvest at La Crau

We are all driving up together in the old Opel, and get as far as Paris, where we swerve into a brick wall on Le Périférique. Some pulling of metal later we free the left front tire. The ride continues under grey overcast, dripping skies, over slippery highways. A couple of hours later we find ourselves on curvy country roads lined with sunflowers turning their heads towards their yellow companion in the sky. Our farming friends greet us with homemade wine and freshly picked fruit. Long evenings begin with singing newly discovered old French folksongs, and end with laying down close to the hearth fire, barely finding our blankets. Dawn wakes our dull, wine-wasted bodies with a plunge into a cold stream, freshly baked bread and horrible French coffee, which gives us just enough strength to stumble towards the orchard, shaking old plum trees and gathering all that falls in big leather bags. Every evening we take crates full of sweet-smelling plums to the dryery, collecting some coins to buy supper and real wine. On the last evening we roast the billy goat over a campfire. We had warned it many times to stop chasing and butting us…

Joep Jilesen

Am I a Boy?

Never before had winter begun in October.
Arctic winds made all life retreat into
The freezing house kept warm with burning coal and
Cigarettes, damaging his infant trachea and lungs.

He spent years of his young life
In hospital rooms with smelly bedpans,
Sweet vanilla pudding as dessert, and
Merciless butt-shots of penicillin.

Often he found reprieve in reading
Picture books with shifting dragonflies and
Sly foxes under his blanket
Until the flashlight's battery ran out.

Regularly a woman in a black laced dress
Visited him in his sterile room.
She stood behind a glass wall, gesturing,
Speaking to the nurse who called her his mother.

One morning the woman came and said:
You are going home with me.
She handed him stripeless strange clothes,
Which fitted awkwardly around his small limbs.

Then she gave him a pair of slippers
And tied the laces.
His feet felt heavy and tight.
All boys wear these shoes, she mentioned.

She held his hand firmly as they walked
Through a hollow-sounding corridor.
The shoes burned and tired his feet.
At the end a door opened into a bright light.

Standing in the sunlight he stared down
At the brown ribbed pants
And black shiny shoes.
Am I a boy now? he asked his mother.

The Kiss Yanna Bat–Adam

Agnes Cartry

Not Too Sweet

I want stones that burn,
I want feelings that unite,
I want roses that prick
So Life isn't too sweet.

That's fair enough, to suffer,
That's how the depth of the pond
Gets its rich emerald
Into my veins, indelibly.

I can see you shun discomfort,
I can see shallow reflections
In the absence of your silence,
I feel who reverberates light.

Do not strangle my spirit
With a bandage fitted for a snake bite,
Do not murder my soul
By washing the gold back out.

Agnes Cartry

Ilaria del Carretto

Now serenely I rest,
My softened lids,
Pale almonds holding
The kernel of my soul,
Blissfully echo
The delicate silence
Suspending the rustle
In the Tuscan olive trees.

I have only uttered gentle melodies
And child-like words.
Pura
I am, my lips have only kissed
Rose petals and children's fingers

My brow never frowned at tyrants,
I retained a placid composure,
Blue like the laguna on a late
Summer morning,
When I witnessed injustice.

No man will ever see my alabaster breast,
Nor witness my throat contract
Under my buttoned corolla.

This I choose
And I am at peace.

Agnes Cartry

Barn by Georgia O'Keeffe

It's a barn she painted
All white
Extending beyond the edge
Of the canvas into golden dunes

The dunes appear to be moving
The barn is so still
And edgeless
Like time

There are no windows
Or rather no walls
Perhaps the windows
Are painted white too

She wanted to convey
That the dunes are alive
Breathe and make love
While the barn will disappear

Agnes Cartry

Pet Triptych

1.
Three stars in the sky
Make a filigree line
One large and shiny
One center jewel of a tree
One tiny like me
Lying on the darkening grass
My head resting on the dog's soft belly

2.
Cat's head sinking in silk blanket
So still so tranquil
One striped paw curled up
One spotted paw turned out
She likes to sleep where my feet would be
I stick them out and she's comfy

3.
Curled black cat
On the yellow shower mat
Takes me by surprise
In the middle of the night
His eyes yellow
His pupils black
More striking
Than a Matisse painting.

Still Life Deborah McKay

St. Bride Kevin Watts

Agnes Cartry

Confession

My Lord,
I would rather call you Creator
And speak without words
But I am here prompted to play
With symbolic glyphs
After burdening meaning
All day for money.

I am still afraid
To say the irrevocable No
That frees my flight to Yes
To Poverty
Like St. Francis
Leaving the too-familiar merchants,
Guarding gold in his soul to be true
To your ministry:

Undistracted dedication
To unveiling beauty,
Revealing the light,
Infusing what is opaque,
Relentlessly being Creator.

John Craig

From *Psalms of Friendship*

Small

There is a peace in little tasks, a reassuring scale
in the cleaning of a room, the weeding of a garden.
Doing what we know we can when we can secures the sense
of being worthy servants prepared for prosperity.

It is the same in our relations with eternity.
The prayer that opens heaven, that drops the ladder to earth
for us to climb, requires no special talent from our lips—
only our resolution to join God in proffered peace.

Something in us thinks transcendence must be grand, dramatic,
bought by taming an earthquake or discovered in the dust
of post-Apocalypse. No. All we can bear of glory
sits on the tips of our noses awaiting our attention.

What in us favors the distortion into grander feats
than we can dare—visions guaranteed to keep us wishing?
Our real work is small; we have the time, the knowledge, the skill.
Let us be reassured in our little rooms: God abides.

Mohsen Auguste Haboush

John Craig

For Everyone

What is suffering but an overabundance of love,
its current blocked by the body's gates—the unmoving chest,
the throat strangled by language, the eyes glazed against the now?

Earthly identity is the distortion of the soul
done by the damming of love. Whatever follows "I am"
is a lie, a vanity, a pillar of salt bent back.

Are you lonely? You are not alone. Your love is the same
as all love. Free it and the fear of death dissolves in air.
Do you demand perfection? Your memory of heaven
makes you proud, resentful of exile in this dirty place.
You call the shame of your desire independence and turn
in fury to make a statue self separate from God.

When we have forsaken all claims to being anything,
the body surrenders, love resumes its flow out of time—
river of everything, awareness of God its current.
Our real work is small; we have the time, the knowledge, the skill.
Let us be reassured in our little rooms: God abides.

John Craig

To Live This Way

One's moments in the world but not of it—discovering
oneself unhitched and free to go but still in the habits
of freighted flesh—are enlightening, poignant, humbling, strange.

One watches one's friends perform, their labored machinery
bound to an unread script. One's body rumbles to take part,
but the soul's unfettered will is strong enough to refuse.

Oh to live this way! This is life after death, floating free
but still generous to the earth, a selfless monitor.
Now the task: how to direct the superabundant love?

Learning this long work—one's astral duties—takes centuries,
but eternity is measured in attention, not time,
as one masters unbounded expansion and contraction.

When I take the hook of a touch, a voice, and am reeled back
to the body, let me not forget the loving duties
of the liberated soul: to be, and hold the mirror.

The Third Call Daniele Scapati

John Craig

If You Weren't

When one suspects that life on earth is too repetitive
and patterned to be real—not a hoax, more a hologram—
then one has arrived at a small separation from it,
and one can no longer act as an entertained player
in the Angels' elaborate sensory game. What now?

One could be like Moses and try to lead people away
from the established order, out through the hole one has made.
Or like Jesus teaching compassion for all who know not
what they do. Or like Muhammed warning that Allah is
not what one thinks, so one had better die before one dies.

But these and every true prophet's alternative vision
amount to the same thing, minus the cultural settings.
So if prophecy is just another loop in the game,
might it not be better to just skip it—the decalogues,
boddhisatva pledges, all the ways—and go straight to God?

What is it all but God anyway? Participation
in God, being God, is all there really is. Believing
in the borders and boundaries of otherness turns us
away from God's unity and make a game of being.
If you weren't a space-time body, God would make perfect sense.

John Craig

Miracles

The lower functions' determination of self-interest
shapes and polishes personality, feeds it, grooms it
till even prayer cannot escape its gravity. Too fat.
If you're fortunate, your prayers will disgust you and you'll stop.
Put away your petitions. Silently let God be God.

To awaken means to be able to observe the world—
all of it—as a manifestation of God acting
without your consultation but with your full acceptance.
Most often, we must be shocked into this miracle state.
From it we see all things are already accounted for.

If you've employed and fully trained a steward in your house,
let him do the praying. He knows the right things to pray for
and doesn't embellish. He'll bring the household's attention
to the brink of the miracle state then retire to watch,
mute and cross-eyed from his small room, the arrival of God.

Then you won't need your obesity anymore, your wit,
the testimonial you angled for, your skill at cards.
God's taken care of it all, and after the sweet visit,
you may note an essence, a perfume, a capacity
of discernment to navigate the path of miracles.

Peter Albert Ana Rodriguez

Museum Auguste Haboush

John Craig

Poverty

Poverty is not the problem. A glut of goods corrodes
the heart worse than a lack of them. Where will we put all this?
Storage for the excess has become a boom industry.

In the choked river of products—coffee mugs, cameras,
assault rifles, stealth bombers, diplomas, building permits,
plastic bags, human bodies—can you find your buried soul?

Can you revive it, resuscitate its lost attention,
breathe for it until it remembers itself and returns
to eternity? If in the end it must discard you,

dead in the garbage, dead on a planet turned inside out,
yet you can be the hero of the soul, the reminder,
the reawakener of this visitor from no place.

How many orbits naked under the merciless sun
will it take to burn away and clean what man has piled up?
How great is the poverty man must relearn to survive.

John Craig

Crossing

There is enough time, time to stop, subtract yourself, step out
of the flow of events and let the stimulations go
without response. They will nuzzle, sigh, beg, pinch and slap you.
Wait them out. There is enough time, enough time to peel off
each stinging thought from the swarm of beliefs your departure
will agitate. Slow your breathing. Above all, do not nod.
Wait for God. God's spark nourishes itself on your silence.

There is enough time, enough time, enough. Eternity
will open around you, above you. You will understand
that all the questions bind you, pull you back into the flow
of mind. You will understand there is nothing to be done
or said or thought. You become as breath, effortless, unowned.
It is clear the life you've left here, life in name and body,
is school for love. You discern you are not alone. Welcome.

Umberto Auguste Haboush

Zoya Dreaming Tina Mlakar

Milena Mlakar

Angel in Disguise

You and I are hiding today
staying under the covers
long quiet Sunday hours
like real princesses
feeling the new moon
through seven mattresses

Your eyes,
dark hazel-chocolate mystery
royal, calm, melancholic sanctuary of sadness
Your silver-beige skin
smooth as warm water
innocence in a face
doesn't tell your Greyhound age

Elevators, storms, noisy places, summer heat,
perhaps some ancient memory of a hand,
that could hit and hurt; perhaps
this brings electric shivers to your feet

But when you run, there's light
a shooting star on the ground; joyous, weightless, fun
Though, I never saw you catch a rabbit.
I wonder why?
I wonder, if you're an angel in disguise?

Huge, penetrating question marks
staring from your soft eyes
straight into mine
are pushing me towards
unanswered corners of my heart

Milena Mlakar

Purple Hope

The songs of rain last night
thunder striking the roof
electricity of the mind blown away

last will lying on the chair

morning fate surprises me again
my story didn't hit the end
a stainless waterpot calls
for my soul to stay home

my human body wrapped in a soft white robe
my doing wants to rest
the dishes, they can wait today
love only fears to be left alone,

unexplored, without purple hope

Spring Melody Takayuki Harada

Milena Mlakar

To a Young Poet

on the other side of this blank page
find your self
loyal to those who hear the voice

in the wilderness
the desert of no-mind
have no more fear to say
I am the one

Try and explore
stepping into the unknown is
not always kind
not always the land of possibilities
or is it ?

The sound of eyelashes closing
pen scratching
make friends with time
Fly
if you have to
but always land new

Claire Walker

A Grain of Sand

They dropped sand in me the day I met you.
It will wash out in a few days, I told myself.
After a week, a month, a year, it did not go away.

Sometimes hurt too much, the heart wants to
take it out but can't—because
it was not put there by her, just like the oyster
didn't choose to let it in.

So the sand takes root, grinds the heart,
And the struggle continues
 between yes and no,
 between should and shouldn't,
 between could and couldn't,
 between sweet and sorrow,
Between "to be" and "not to be."

Will a pearl appear one day?
Half exhausted and half hoping, I dare not ask.
It is already here, They tell me,
Right in the sand.
They came together, as a gift for you.

Daniele Petrini

At Pomposa

translated from the Italian by Stefano Petrizzo

At Pomposa the fog is inside the walls
If you go there when the sky is blue
it feels like you're inside an error
You're walking in a mistake, a parenthesis

From a similar route precise images
and sounds came to us one evening,
tempered on each side

As if they'd escaped from a prison

An abbey so beautiful at sunset
it risks becoming a lie—
you look and forget yourself, and yet
it fills you with that which awakens you:

the light, the singing, the community
All more than elsewhere, more
moment, more minute, more second

And you a breath, only a breath:

but so near.

Sutter Buttes Agnes Lendech

Stefano Petrizzo

Envoy

Go out into the world but be careful,
do not fall into the hands of cynics or rednecks,
do not stop to gab with tourists, but walk straight to my lover.

And when you come upon beggars with elaborate signs,
innocent gypsy boys, grasp tight the pearls in your pocket.

Go along the store windows and glance at your reflection—
it is good to be reminded of your slouching posture, your loss of hair,
it is good to see yourself and not to wince or turn away in disgust.

But pass by the suits of Gucci, the lizard-skin shoes with abalone inlay.

People will come to you and ask is this the way
to Murray Street? They will hand you a placard

advertising foot massage, they will try to sell you flowers

stolen from the cemetery, or unload on you some hot cell-phones—or worse

fake Prada handbags!

At this point refrain, ignore them and keep your focus
on the road ahead. Just walk and look, allow no thought to enter
the narrow gate, the eye of the needle you've shaped yourself into.

Let them knock at the door, let them pound, let them
fall on their knees on the sidewalk in tears, but don't let them in.

Continue sure and straight on your road,
be it grimy and strewn with flattened chewing gum
or dusty and drought-stricken or shattered by war or natural disaster.

Though tsunamis visit your boxed-in shorelines,
turn away and keep on past the fallen, the evening silhouette
of the lawnmower, the trash can overturned.

You have not so far to go. You will know when you round
the corner and see her stoop.

And when she buzzes you in, and when you are standing
in front of her door, don't think about the words you are going to say.

I have adorned you well. When the time comes,
when my lover opens the door, look her straight

in the eye—that's it, look.

Toits Hughes Chevalier

Stefano Petrizzo

The Holy One

We supposed some things were better left unsaid,
but when we looked it was hard to say which.
The cold eyeball of the news, the territories
of refracted light, a corn on my left toe. These things
didn't seem to matter. But goddammit something firm
under my feet would have helped!
For once we wanted to bump our heads
against something other than air.
Even an idea, but a good one,
would have made more impact
if we could have held it in our hands like a ball
or a piece of fruit, a glass, an ax handle, anything
you could really get your hand around and know
for certain that you had something.
But these were hard times of leisure and luxury.
No one was marching you to the wall of dawn,
setting up a provisional camp in your back yard.
Shrapnel was a star you wore on your forehead yes,
but just a word. How dangerous could that be?
We were recumbent, too relaxed in our angst,
too settled in restlessness. No one
would have admitted. No one would have said it.
There were flowers out the window, yellow tulips,
and the grass was wet and green, cold and cloud.
But who would look? Who would admit this freshness?

Stefano Petrizzo

Elegy

When did I lose you?
I never really had you

but must always grope
toward your possibility.

To say *hand, river, child*
seems simple, a person or

thing. There's too much
fullness for you to appear

as that which is called,
named, that I should feel

the hollow of something
missing. If I just said *man*,

or for example, *father*,
you would come out

of the nondescript forest. Be.
Only then could I lose you

Stefano Petrizzo

On Looking at Leonardo's Lady with an Ermine and Seeing My Situation

She wants vacations, Cecilia.
What would you know about that?

Your life is a vacation, posing for portraits,
your oversized hand, the oversized beast.

I have only to raise my eyes
from the grasping instinct of its eyes,

climb the ladder of beads from your breast
to the chopping block of your chin,

over the slightly tight-lipped mouth
and nose like the long stem of a backward

leaning Y to your open wide-set eyes,
and I know I don't need an island beach,

a table at the café in the piazza,
or even a new drug.

I am open to the cold raw cave.

Stefano Petrizzo

Bare Trees in Morning Fog

This one just out the window, the branches a child's
scribbles, for years now half dead, asking
more than the others.

What is missing in the ground around its roots?
Phosphorus? Potassium?

It stays half alive, one foot
on this side, one foot on the other.
It must know something we don't.

We can only offer a leftover bowl
of rice, a crust of bread
into the dark, holding on

to the belief or half-belief that some nourishment
will pass over.

But the tree bears signs
of the passage, like Christ taken down from the cross,
like Lazarus.

Jo Anna Mortensen

Four Portraits

Alexander Gardner's photo of Lincoln with cracked plate, 1865

Bushy eyebrows arc beneath
the four furrows on his brow;
deep creases frame his mouth—
then cut down into his short prickly beard.
His bowtie's cockeyed and off-center.
The weariness biting his bones, embraced.

Meher Baba during seclusion at Meherabad, 1941

Baba stands at the open window—
potent, quiet, collected.
His forehead and arm
dissolve into sunlight.
Long hair spills over his white gauzy gown;
dark shadows at his back hint of a door.
In Baba's silence there's no division;
he gives and receives light.

Rembrandt last self-portrait, 1669, Mauritshuis

Quick brushstrokes dash across the hat,
silver to ochre then green to gold—
puffs of hair drift below like clouds at sunset.
With Saskia, Hendrickje, and Titus gone
Rembrandt's hushed, prepared. His gaze
peers out even now
from his putty face.

Leonardo self-portrait, circa 1510

Fine lines drawn in red chalk,
thick brows shield deep set eyes,
gravity tugs on his lips.
Leonardo's beard ripples
like a meandering stream
or the mane of an ancient god.
He awakes to find
the world asleep
yet affirms that everything
is connected to everything.

Meher Baba Candice Goldman

Lu Pan and His Teacher Anthony Emmolo

Jo Anna Mortensen

The Red Skiff and the Swan

walking along the Rhine
fantastic clouds above
swiftly changing shapes
bitter wind against the skin
large barges with colorful cargo
easing downstream
people passing on the path
wrapped in coats, striped scarves
pushing prams or hurrying home
bundles tucked under arms
suddenly a cherry red skiff appears
long and thin
its lone oarsman silently
strokes the water
and then from the riverbank
lumbering down the slope
as a waking bear might
a white swan slips into the silvery water
swims towards the skiff
lifts suddenly out of the Rhine
and follows the boat like
an angel painting blue shadows
in the river

Jo Anna Mortensen

When He Wakes Me

his breath's an invisible river
skipping across the sea
whispering in poplars
splitting on the swallow's wings

his wrath snaps and scatters trees
rips farmhouses from foundations
churning landscapes, slapping waves
while sailors pray or curse him

his limbs spiral out from the sun
like a pinwheel
corral clouds against the mountains
sprinkle seeds in the ditch

when he wakes me
I rise from this body
my breath unites with his
I don't know if I'm spirit
or a dream

Jo Anna Mortensen

Women on the Outskirts of Anchorage

We don't lock our doors.
Bring us silver-scaled fish;
we know how to gut them.
We read Hemingway.
Bring us Russian vodka.
We'll make Bloody Marys
with celery and Tabasco.
Buy us sable coats.
We don't go to church.
We dig for clams and
run like hell from rip tide.
Pass the Lucky Strikes.
We trade recipes and miseries
but we don't backbite.
Come summertime,
we don't mind if
the kids run wild 'til midnight.
Winter—out they go
skating after supper.
When school starts up
we can't wait
to pop champagne;
swarm into June's living room,
laughing. Dinner ready
right at six; toys picked up.
We don't complain to our men
except dark days when
we're stark raving mad.

Green Tatyana Polovinko

Jo Anna Mortensen

We Sometimes Wake

The world is always waiting. Night fades;
Eos opens an apricot gate.
The call of a mourning dove rises,
followed by the she-dove's answer,
her four notes high. A peony petal
falls like a silk parachute drifting in horizontal flight.
The world is waiting, keen to meet us and
we sometimes wake to green's extravagance,
nibbling on tidbits of April light.

Jo Anna Mortensen

Solar Winds

I want a room in the inner court of the palace
I want to hear the sea whisper to stars
I want to release the white dove
and join the clapping children.

Let the thrush's trill ache inside me
and the fire blaze without crackling.
Tangle my past into purple kelp
or plant it beneath the foxglove's shadow.

I still see electric green blue—
shimmering, astonishing darkness.
When an angel paints your face,
there's no way to erase the marks.
But do not command the heart;
let it be a weather vane for solar winds.
Forget my name and face
but not my slender fingers.

Erika Charles Frank

Conversation Auguste Haboush

Tzvi Schmilovich

A Starbuck's Meditation

The man is taken by his screens. He may be getting
word, important news from the beyond.

He could be a devotee contemplating the everlasting.
Or a master examining his path in the marketplace.

He must be internally calm though seemingly agitated—
a proof of a supreme self control.

He shoots me an angry look; no doubt testing my psychic mettle.
He relishes the decadent beverage, has an eyeful of the exciting girl…

—he could be breaking up with purity, kind of jumping the monastery wall
seeking fresh, rousing revelations. Or else practicing redemption

through the gutter; ah, that's why he's loud, obnoxious on the phone!
On the other hand he may be an adherent to the doctrine

of personal salvation by filling oneself to the brim
worshiping the world as a bottomless well;

by hook or by crook non-stop having the cup full—
there he goes for a refill

Tzvi Schmilovich

Down the Road

When the pool of stillness locked
on me its forest-eye

I entered free of intention.
Now lifeless prizes, glittering bones

clamor and eye me
through their holes.

When did the venture turn into a hunting expedition?
When I couldn't keep up

with the route, weighed down
by the trophies I hauled home?

Here I lie in wait for
another occasion.

Tzvi Schmilovich

How to Write a Villanelle

Take a serious break, stop everything;
that's how great things have started.
Loosen up, and pour yourself a drink

to stir up an inspired think
for what's to be poetically treated.
Take a dedicated break, stop everything.

If you don't get far, like me here on the brink
of the third stanza, which has coincided
with an empty glass—pour the second drink,

it'll no doubt open a creative spring;
tapped—you'll be blissfully flooded.
Wait patiently, stop everything.

If the method doesn't yet bring
anything good—may be you aren't that gifted
or it's time for one more drink.

Nothing? Silence? Could be a good thing
at least, relieved that this here has ended—
take a serious break, stop everything,
loosen up, and pour yourself a drink.

Landscape Elle van Glabbeek

Judith Grace

In the Mauve Clover

Bumblebees grazing in the mauve clover;
Crisscrossing coppery spears and lithe
Silver grasses waving their parchment pennants;
Fallen branches grown over with lichen
Alive with lizards and the hovering of gnats;
Tufts of yellow dandelions in tattered ruffs
Purple arabesques on curling tendrils
And gray balding milkweeds in the dense
Green bed spangled with wild pink sweetpeas—
All patterned with light and shade from the overhanging leaves
Genuflecting drowsily as the wind sweeps over
The tangle of weeds, woven thicker than the carpets of Tabriz

Judith Grace

Sunday

I hear church bells ringing from a mile away
How is it I never heard them before?
After all, it's Sunday

The sun's balancing on the tip of midday
The sky is a revolving door
I hear church bells ringing from a mile away

I've been thinking of nothing to do all day
And every one of my pockets is poor
After all, it's Sunday

My widowed shadow's gone astray
He won't be stalking me anymore
I hear church bells ringing from a mile away

Maybe I shall stop here and pray
Lying upside-down on this grassy floor
After all, it's Sunday

There's no one now I need to obey
I'm a white wave falling onto a blue shore
I hear church bells ringing from a mile away
After all, it's Sunday

Judith Grace

This Morning

The glass on the night table suddenly felt itself brimming with water
That had arrived after ferrying millions of years from earth to clouds
And the window-sill, that it was flooded with acres of ancient light
Overjoyed, the curtains realized that they were open
To let the sky of the Genesis enter in
The damask chair was not waiting to be filled
But thrilled deliciously in its own firmness
The rose bud picked last night suddenly understood everything that has ever been known
About opening
And the walls knew the peace they had always held
Tenderly between their arms for the first time

Ocean Elle van Glabbeek

Judith Grace

The Sea That Day

Delicious sand under feet
Waves supple and blue
Couple holding and loving each other
Yellow sun disk rising like a child's balloon
Seven birds flying off to heaven
Striped beach chairs arrayed to infinity

Wind flapping through the banner
Kissing me the wind, kissing me
The sun, kissing me the music
Kissing me the birds, kissing me the people
The waves are kissing me and the sands
Are kissing me

Sea turning soft somersaults onto the shore
Its acquiescent lover under the blue-eyed sky
Tiny boat in the distance floating away

Judith Grace

Titian's Last Painting

Not the *Deposition* painted at 98 when he was almost blind,
But the unknown *Resurrection* painted at 102 when he was completely blind
He knew by feeling where to draw the lines
Like Beethoven, deaf, who heard the half-sounds
Filling them in with thick impasto strokes that were braille when he ran his
Fingers over them
The Risen Christ may have been a portrait himself
He wasn't sure if it was young or old
Or if the stigmata had healed
Or if the smile was triumphant or meek
He didn't know how to paint in the angels thronging to greet the Body of Gold
So he feathered in wings like the wings he heard beating around his head
Trusting now that paint was light

Judith Grace

Spell

Drink of the unpeeled indigo grape
Spit the seeds out and bind around
Your forehead its fire-lobed leaves
Let the hummingbird fly backwards through your mind
The insects prick your ankles
The birds enter their birdhouse
To shelter somewhere in your heart
Lay the amber hills across your body like a bandage
Layer in the geraniums, the forked palm leaves
Shadows and mid-summer light—
Let me be filled with you only
World of quiet lakes and terraced fields...

William Page

August Moon

You sat with your legs apart, fanning yourself;
on your face beads of sweat glistened in the light.
You wanted to wait until dark to make love,
but the sultry day had turned into a sultry night.

You were hoping for a breeze and complained
that the window was shut, but I said you were wrong.
I stood and went to the casement and leaned out
to show that it had been open all along.

Outside the evening swallowed up the garden's shade,
and the black tree trunks grew blacker still.
Then a crow's caw sounded above us like a short laugh,
and a barn owl flew up over a hill.

A red moon was pulling itself up over a meadow
like a pregnant woman lifting herself from a bed,
and the humid, shadowy heat lay
heavily on the lawn like a marker for the dead.

When I turned, your hand, my love, without the license
of your will, had started to unbutton your dress,
and you, who ordinarily look so girlish,
stood and stared at me like a barbarian princess.

Beauty of Wings Takayuki Harada

William Page

Voices in the Wind

You who inhabit this land that was our home,
speak no more of us with the sad regret
of those you have surpassed, speak no more
of us as those whose sun has long been set.

The yellowed parchments that crack and crumble
in the care of your warm, anxious hands
tell little of the heartache we felt, of lost love,
or of the splendor of our summer grasslands.

What you know of us does not sweeten
the grapes in our vineyards, now overgrown;
it doesn't include our memories of storms in April,
or include all the seeds that in our time were sown.

What you know of us does not tell how
in the fields in summer we rested in the shade
to drink water or to hear a song, sung by a girl,
or to sit and watch as our children played.

Your history of us is not as telling
as we had hoped; it does not rise above
the page to steer your thoughts from your thoughts
to the crucial question of how to love.

Your geography is more human.
With its forests of trees and cliffs of stone,
it is hesitant, almost nostalgic, in its
remembrance of the dust that was our bones.

We were more adventurous than you supposed.
Coming before you, you are what we foretold.
Coming before you, we know what it is to be young
and arrogant and what it means to grow old.

We watch now, scanning the domain we created,
remembering how we once too had faces,
remembering how time bound us to this land.
We were here once, we were once in your place.

We were once more to the world than voices
in the wind, more in the scheme of your line of time
than forgotten souls honored by stones inscribed
with forgotten names and a verse or two of rhyme.

William Page

Divan 24

A few pines. Some Manzanita.
A mountain in the distance. A sun.
A landscape to rebuild and renew.
A soil of red dust and orange rock.
A dream of Ithaca.

Here, we thought to finally rest,
to build for our children a legacy
of an earth worth preserving.
We labored, but already we were
thinking of the next adventure,
already we were enfolding our selves
into the distances of a sea
that leaped and washed below
a sky of evolving planets and stars.
Already we found time to set our tools aside
and ask if our failures
weren't more heartfelt than the successes
we were so eager to name.

And if, in the daring our task, we overshot
the caliber of our abilities, what of it?

Our hands have learned humility;
our arms and legs, to be alive;
our thoughts, the burden of the gods;
our spirits, to survive.

Male Nudes Jonathan Beth

William Page

Divan 5

Do not concern yourself
with the lizards that scamper over the rocks
and dart through the dried grass,
they will find stillness in the heat.
The summer has no need of fences,
and the sun does not care if it is yellow,
but the cows have left the golden field
for the green grass by the canal.
Are you thinking of yourself?

Do not grieve for the man
with the black disposition:
the night will send him a lover;
or for the woman with the yellow thoughts:
the morning sun will be her friend.
Do not grieve for the mute boy:
the crickets in the evening will be his voice,
or for the girl who speaks to the river
and is amazed by the sea:
her neighbors will give her
water from their well to drink.
Do not grieve for the one
who is looking for his shoes
among the Manzanita and the poison oak,
or for the one who couldn't find
the north star in the pond
at the bottom of the road:
they will find each other.

Who has found his conscience
while surrounded by injustice?
Who knows pain without bitterness?
The rose has climbed up its stem of thorns,
and the tyrant has only oppressed himself,
and the man who has transformed
the injustice of being a man
will walk in the shadow of his soul.
Are you still thinking of yourself?

Stanley Fligner

Caterpillar's Delight

I race down the woods 'twixt the bright mountain springs,
While sav'ring the fragrance the morning mist brings.
I light on a leaf as a drop of dew clings
In a sun-riched heav'n where the marigold sings.
I measure my life now in butterfly wings.

Good Day Linda Carter Holman

Stanley Fligner

To John Who Aged with Grace

When inside time the sea o'erwhelmed the land
As waves and waves crashed harsh upon the shore,
The steadfast pier collapsed onto the sand,
Its pieces grasped away and seen no more,

When hordes of winds invad'd the wintered trees,
As needles fled the pines before the sounds,
Our graceful oak that beckoned sky with ease
Had giant limb lean cracked upon the ground,

When you who in your youth held audience
With poise and skill belonged to you alone,
Had arms and legs once spoke the perfect dance
Forget their lines as if were never known,

You held yourself akin as can to one
Who countered tide, time, battered pride as one.

Samuel Provenzano

The Accordionist

Francisco:

My name is Francisco Esparta, and I've been playing accordion for thirty-three years. I play mostly music from my homeland, which is Spain, but I love gypsy music from all cultures, so I sometimes play my favorite gypsy melodies from memory. I've played for parties, weddings, and at restaurants, but lately I've been playing in the streets of New York for anyone who likes my playing. People often leave me tips and make requests of music they wish to hear. Many of the requests are American tunes, which I've never heard. They leave me tips anyway.

Lately a dog has begun to follow me home after I've been playing. He is a medium-sized dog, and he is gold with black whiskers. I live on the second floor of a building; it is an apartment above a grocery store. When I look out my window, down at the street below after I've been playing all day, the dog is gone. But he shows up to where I play each day, and he sits by my side quietly when I play. He seems to enjoy the sound of the accordion and the music it makes. Though I don't play in the same place each day, the dog continues to find me, and he waits patiently until I'm finished for the day.

Corazon:

My friend who has passed away called me Corazon. He was a dear friend who gave me food and shelter for all the years we were together. He played music on a box-shaped thing like this stranger plays. It gives me peace to hear this music again. Sometimes I cry at night because I miss my friend so much.

This stranger seems to know and play the same songs my friend used to play. It has brought me new happiness to be able to hear these sounds again. I wish I could tell the stranger how grateful I am for reminding me that we have much to live for. The other day, when this new stranger finished for the day, as he packed up, he reached out his hand to me and when I drew close, he patted my head. No one has patted my head in such a long time and, though I was afraid and I felt a growl in my throat, I let him pet me. He gave me a piece of cheese and a hunk of bread. I watched the stranger's eyes, and it seemed to me he was very kind. He spoke to me gently and though I didn't understand the words, I'm sure he intended to be my friend. I thanked him with a lick on his hand. After he wiped his hand on his pants, he patted my head again.

Francisco:

Today, as I played in a new location, there was a larger group of people than usual who stopped to hear me play. One man set his hat upside down on the ground before me, and people began to fill the hat with not only coins but paper bills as well.

The dog watched as people stepped forward and placed the money in the hat. He seemed to understand because he wagged his tail each time some one new gave money. Many of the people seemed happy; the sun was shining. One young couple began to dance, and then another, and before long, there were many couples dancing to my music.

The dog became very excited as he watched the people dance and at one point, he began to make a high-pitched sound in his throat. It did not sound like an angry sound or a bark, but like an attempt to sing with my music. What made it so special was that he seemed to be listening closely enough to be in tune with the music. When I looked at him, I swear he seemed to be smiling. As I listened to his sounds, I found myself humming audibly with him. After the tune was over, a young woman stepped out of the crowd and placed a plastic bowl of water before him. He went to it and drank the entire bowl.

Corazon:

My new friend played even more beautifully today, and people were dancing. I found myself singing along with his melodies, and he began singing too. When I followed my friend home tonight, after his performance, he invited me into his home. I was reluctant at first, but he insisted and once inside, he gave me a bowl of water and a bowl of food, which was delicious. I didn't realize how hungry I was. After I ate and drank my fill, he sat on the floor next to me and patted me. He spoke softly to me until I fell asleep. I slept better than I had slept in a long time. It was a relief to be off the streets and safe.

When I awoke the next morning, my new friend let me out and, soon after, he came outside with his music box, and I followed him to a busy street corner where he played for people passing by. Many people, who seemed to be in such hurry one moment, stopped abruptly when they heard him play. The faces of those who listened changed dramatically after a few moments. People seemed less frantic and more at peace, and the transformation was almost immediate. One of the passers by, a beautiful young woman with fire-red hair and laughing dark eyes, came to me and gave me a delicious bone, and she said my name.

Francisco:

Last night, I brought the dog inside. He was very well mannered and, though he seemed a little uncertain at first, he soon made himself at home. I'm not sure how long he had lived in the streets, but he seems very grateful for every small kindness. I'm finding that his companionship has given new meaning to my life. I'm beginning to understand the "best friend" concept. When I look into his eyes, I see an ever growing trust as well as something I'm a little afraid to name. It's as though he reads my thoughts. He requires nothing of me, but he is constantly focused on me.

Last evening, as we were finishing up for the day, an attractive red-haired woman brought a huge bone to the dog. As he gently took it from her, she came to me.

"You have a beautiful dog," she said. "What's his name?"

Her question stopped me; it had never occurred to me to name the dog or that he was "my" dog. In fact, I thought of him as my equal, and neither of us belonged to each other, but rather, we were friends who found each other.

"He's a stray," I said. "I haven't named him yet. What do you think I should name him?" Her eyes sparkled as she thought for a moment.

"Well," she said, "his eyes are very emotional, so he has a lot of heart and you look and sound Spanish. How about something Spanish and passionate, Corazon?

Irishman Auguste Haboush

The dog's ears immediately stood upright.

"Ah, yes," I said. "Corazon is the perfect name for him. He seems to like it as well."

Corazon:

The woman with the red hair came to my friend's home tonight carrying a bag. She prepared dinner for my friend and they shared their food with me. I heard my friend call the woman Rose. I still wonder how she knew my name. Rose called my friend Francisco. After we all ate, they asked me to sit and then they asked me to shake hands with them. They laughed as I obeyed each of their commands. At one point, I had to relieve myself, so I scratched at the door. They praised me and patted me and then they let me out. When I finished, I scratched at the door, and they let me in.

I sat in a corner as they drank red liquid from long-stem glasses. Francisco took out his music box and began to play, and Rose removed a black box from her purse and assembled a long tubular musical instrument; she began to play music with Francisco, and it was so lovely, I began to sing. When we were done, Francisco said we were the Corazon trio. I thought then, and I believe now, that humans could be so much more than they are if they could just stop trying to be so many things that they're not. My heart felt full. I found myself lying down with my head between my front paws.

Max Meyers

When First

when first I saw you
I was struck
striking
captivated
questions filled the air
then when first our eyes met
there was nothing else
the rest of the room melted
time and season froze in the instant
something stirred
something touched
the ensuing smile from your face
such radiance
and I now the willing captive
offer my heart to you

Max Meyers

Day by Day

crossing the waters day by day
astounded, abstracted, balanced
engulfed in the moment serene
my eyes trace the silver edging of the clouds breathing softly wind
across my face lost in you

The Sacred Source Angela Tuccinardi

Max Meyers

One

I catch myself being
at one with all and everything
knowing nothing sensing so much
one soul one breath, breathing
one eternal cast of love
continuously in stillness moving
waving thru hearts and eyes and leaves and beaks and water and wind and wood and soil and stone my fingers pulse with the beating flow of life
barely holding back the tears
filled with grace and honored living flesh now witness drawing new breath ever one with God

Max Meyers

In Awe

standing in absolute awe—how could this possibly be?
this beautiful world, this miraculous fact of being, such a gift,
though gift is too light of a term to be a measure, for the
miraculous, inexplicable, unfathomable manifestation of existence.
what then the duty? for this surely is not a frivolous happenstance
these sensations, these thoughts, these resonances with creation!
how so and by what intent have we come forth to be in this glorious
instant o wonder of wonders to see what has been given this could not
be less than love, and such love bestowed without clamor although so
announced in spectacular, breathtaking abundance endlessly becoming,
becoming, becoming and travelers all, we who abide here one need query
the task at hand for it must lead somewhere as one must carry the
gathered sum of being to that end as well so that understanding be
true and generously thankful and this life, this profound gift, not be
wasted.

Dante and Virgil Riding Geryon Angela Tuccinardi

Max Meyers

Enough

there is an ethereal wisp
subtle in voiceless sweetness
a caring understanding of emptiness
worn like gossamer wings
born of being enough

In the Middle of the Journey Angela Tuccinardi

Francis Knoll

Mystic Waltz

It is as if the music came up from the grave.
Ineffable transparent echoes long lost
Skimming our orbs with heavenly voices
Crying out, thrust, then eventually tossed
Upon nescient ears unaware but unashamed
To hear, to feel, and to enter it untamed.

Petals of sound with mild fragrance perfumed;
Intoxicatingly delicious for our hearts to consume.
Taking us now down to that stopped silence chained
From which this sound was only lately exhumed.

Martin Dace

The Girl Who Was Not a Vampire

Myrtle had freckles, huge glasses with pebble lenses, and a terrible secret. She was also hopelessly infatuated with the bad boy of the class, Zigmond Bloodfang.

Actually most of the boys in the class were bad, except Freddy Märchen. Freddy was sweet-natured and had a loving heart, which is why the other boys used to set on him in the boys' toilet, push his head into the toilet bowl and pull the chain.

As for Zigmond, or Ziggy to his friends, he was the worst bad boy and he barely deigned to notice Myrtle's existence. Unlike some of the bad boys, he didn't wear a wide silk cravat round his neck. This might turn out to be a significant plot detail, then again, it might not.

Ziggy had a nonchalant grin that was calculated to send a frisson through any girl, starting with her toes and traveling towards her head via various other anatomical sites en route. He used it on Cynthia Moonbreath and she got the frisson right in the pit of her stomach. A less steely-hearted girl would have imagined she was in love. Since Cynthia was beautiful and knew it, she did not fall in love, but merely dived into her desk for an antacid tablet which she kept there for just such eventualities. On emerging again she flicked her raven hair behind her strangely luminous face and smiled at him ambiguously. Ziggy's grin faded because he knew he wasn't the boss any more.

"I want you to beg me for it," he thought.

"I know you want me to beg you for it," she thought. "Too bad."

Myrtle looked on in anguish, wanting him so badly. Clearly to attract a boy you have to be nonchalant like that, and then ambiguous.

"Or if not him then I would settle for one of the other bad boys," she thought, "or in fact any boy, except Freddy, who is not a bad boy at all." What was it about bad boys that made them attractive?

"What should I do?" Myrtle asked her best friend Felicity. Felicity was black and comely, as it says in the Good Book (Song of Solomon 1:5). She loved Myrtle for who she was, neither because of nor despite her freckles and pebble lenses.

"Boys like a challenge," Felicity said. "You have to be nonchalant and then ambiguous."

Myrtle tried being nonchalant for several days and Ziggy didn't notice her at all, so she never got to the ambiguous part.

In the corridor on the way to maths class Freddy asked her about the diagonal in a square homework question, but she was so busy being nonchalant that she just said,

"Square root of two." She didn't see his eyes full of wonder. Felicity saw Freddy's eyes full of wonder, but she thought it was because he was awed by Myrtle's grasp of surds.

"Did you see Freddy's eyes full of wonder?" she asked Myrtle.

"Freddy is sweet," was all Myrtle replied.

'But what was Myrtle's terrible secret?' I hear you ask. As it happens Felicity was to find it out the very next day.

"You know of course that every young teenager is either a vampire or a werewolf these days?" Myrtle said.

Felicity nodded in apparent agreement, her lips pursed. It was a sunny day and they were sitting on the lawn at the back of the school, out of earshot of anyone else. In the distance two figures were in a furtive embrace, and a keen eye might have thought it was Cynthia and Ziggy. A keener eye might have seen Cynthia love-biting Ziggy's neck in a reversal of the time-honored vampire tradition, and Ziggy looking pale with two streaks of blood running down from Cynthia's kiss.

Let us not dwell on the question of whether Ziggy was a virgin, nor speculate on what might happen to Cynthia if he wasn't. There was a school sick room and we shall leave all that unpleasantness to the school nurse to sort out if the occasion arises. She is paid to do that.

"Well..." Myrtle faltered.

Felicity looked with a mixture of anxiety and hope at Myrtle, not daring to guess what Myrtle might say next, because in her heart she sensed something of what it might be. Myrtle turned to make eye-contact with her friend and held both of Felicity's hands.

"Promise never to tell?"

"I promise." Felicity did not blink. Myrtle squeezed her hands.

"I... I'm not a vampire and I'm not a werewolf." She stopped, scanning her friend's face for a reaction.

Felicity said nothing at first. There was a moment's hesitation then she flung her arms around her friend's neck and hugged her. With her mouth close to Myrtle's ear she whispered, "I'm not a vampire or a werewolf either. I'm actually a wood-nymph. Don't tell anyone."

Myrtle pulled back, her eyes wide. "No, I mean, I'm not anything. I'm not even a dryad.
I'm not magic at all."

Felicity recoiled. How could such a thing happen? How could a girl who was not magic in any way have got into school undetected, living all this time unsuspected among teenage vampires and werewolves?

There had always been talk of some dark secret in Nosferatu Academy, something or someone who did not belong and whose presence threatened everything the Academy stood for. Could it be that behind Myrtle's strange appearance lurked a being horribly, insatiably normal?

"Perhaps you are a mermaid?" Felicity suggested. "I know you are very shy about being seen in the shower after games."

"Not even that." Myrtle spoke in a barely audible whisper.

Now Felicity knew the truth. An ordinary person in their midst, and it was her own best friend. She turned her head away and started to gag, at first uncontrollably, but with an effort mastered herself and turned back to face Myrtle, her face a strange color.

"You…" she faltered.

"I… I can't help being me!" Myrtle cried, rivers of tears coursing down her cheeks. "I didn't choose not to be magic!" She buried her face in her hands and sat motionless, occasional sobs shaking her body.

Felicity sat there, stunned, for what seemed an hour but must have been less. Somewhere a long way off a cry was heard, and a girl could be seen running from the bushes clutching her neck. Then emerged a girl with a luminous face and raven hair sauntering across the lawn with a strange smile playing about her lips, which seemed unusually red. Cynthia could accomplish a lot in one break-time.

At last Felicity's hand stretched towards Myrtle and tentatively touched Myrtle's shoulder.

"We've always been friends," she said. "Perhaps… perhaps something can be done. I could take you to Dr. Frankenstein. He might be able to help."

Myrtle looked up and saw Felicity's face through a haze of tears. "No," she said emphatically. "Accept me as I am, or go away."

Felicity said nothing. Perhaps she understood what it was to be the odd one out. After all, most vampires are pale and she was accepted only on sufferance. What might happen if they found out she was only a wood-nymph she dreaded to think.

The bell went and the girls stood up. As they walked back to class, Felicity reached out for Myrtle's hand and held it. There ahead of them was Freddy. He turned and smiled at Myrtle. For the first time she didn't inwardly recoil. Freddy was sweet, not exciting like the other boys. But there was one thing special about him, and that was that he smiled at her, today. Somehow that mattered, right now. She didn't even care that his hair was wet.

"Square root of two," Freddy said. "I like surds, don't you?"

"Not really," Myrtle replied, and then wished she'd said something else. Freddy blushed, turned and walked on, gazing at the floor.

As they entered the classroom Myrtle could see Ziggy sitting at his desk, tilting his chair on its back legs and trying to look cool. But there was something lacking. His grin was more forced and he looked pale. His eyes looked empty. And unlike earlier in the day a wide silk cravat concealed his neck.

Even in her state of anguish Myrtle noticed this detail. She looked around and saw that quite a lot of the boys and some of the girls wore silk scarves too. More than she remembered. But not Freddy. Cynthia turned to smile at Freddy, who looked confused but tried to smile back. Cynthia continued to stare at him and locked her gaze into his. Then she pointed to him and back to herself, slowly and deliberately. "After school," she mouthed.

"Cynthia is running out of victims," Felicity whispered into Myrtle's ear. If it was possible for Myrtle's face to look more anguished than before, it did.

All eyes were to the front as Dr Finsternis rapped his knuckles on the teacher's desk for the start of the lesson on the construction of pentagrams for nefarious purposes.

"The theoretical appreciation of pentagrams involves surds," he said. "You all know how much you enjoy surds." And he gave an amused grimace as the class groaned.

After class Freddy was first to leave since his desk was nearest the door, and Myrtle and Felicity got stuck behind a crowd of other students all pushing and shoving. That's what happens if you are not a naturally pushy person. Somewhere in the middle of the crowd was Cynthia, looking serene in a disturbing way as was her wont. She would certainly make it through the door before they did.

Myrtle grabbed Felicity's wrist. "What shall we do?" she asked. Felicity needed no further explanation, and she pulled Myrtle into the crowd, pushing forward as best as she could. However it made no difference in this bestial melee and they were the last to leave the classroom. Cynthia was a long way ahead of them, almost floating down the corridor as if in no hurry, and Freddy was nowhere to be seen.

They ran on. Somehow, although Cynthia did not run, it was impossible to catch up with her. Myrtle felt as if she were in one of those dreams in which your legs seem to move but you cannot run, and whatever fate is about to engulf you gets closer and closer until you wake up. There was something not quite right going on, something a wood-nymph's magic was insufficient to deal with.

Felicity turned and dragged Myrtle with her. "Round the back!" she hissed. The two friends ran back down the corridor, out through the little gap in the gothic stonework and into the herb garden, making a short cut through mandrakes, henbane and black hellebores. Here was where the school kept its garden of venomous vegetables.

Over in the corner weeds had established themselves too—a clump of tall stems with little globes of white flowers that exploded like fireworks. Someone had been in there and picked a few. Then on through the back entrance to the alchemy laboratory, past luminous blue retorts and bubbling amber liquids and out the other side. Panting in the doorway, they could see the tall clipped hedges that formed the school's maze of vegetable battlements, places where moonstruck girls had sometimes been hunted by werewolves. The sun was setting and the place was falling into twilight. There, glimpsed somewhere behind a leafy wall, were two figures in a topiary arch. One was tall with raven hair framing a luminous face with bright red lips, and the other was shorter, a boy. The boy was holding a bunch of flowers—tall stems with little globes of white flowers that exploded like fireworks. The girl was bending towards the boy's neck.

"Freddy!" Myrtle shouted.

At first nothing happened. The girl's face hovered next to Freddy's neck unmoving. Then slowly she straightened up and turned towards where Myrtle's voice had come from. The boy hardly moved at all. Then the girl walked away and disappeared somewhere inside the maze. In the distance they heard a strangled gurgling sound like someone being sick.

"Freddy!" Myrtle half cried, half sobbed.

Freddy turned and smiled. He made his way through paths this way and that until he was once again outside the maze. Slowly he walked towards the two friends. Myrtle smiled a little too, then her smile disappeared. Freddy's neck was concealed under a silk cravat.

Still smiling, although now with a tinge of worry, Freddy handed the flowers to Myrtle. "For you," he said, a little doubtfully. Myrtle took them, her face a blank. The flowers had a kind of jubilant beauty, she thought distractedly. She gave one to Felicity to look at. Freddy stood there like a statue, not sure what to do next.

How long they would have stood there in silence I do not know. Suddenly Felicity could stand it no longer. "Freddy!" she said, "Why are you wearing a cravat?"

"Oh that!" Freddy said. "I knew Cynthia was up to no good so I dug up a piece of garlic from the herb garden and wrapped it in a cravat round my neck. Cynthia hates garlic, you know."

"So... so she didn't bite you?" Myrtle asked.

With that Freddy pulled the cravat from his neck. His neck was unmarked.

"Oh!" Myrtle exclaimed.

"Now I know something about you," Freddy said, and this time his eyes twinkled mischievously.

"What?" Myrtle asked nervously.

He lowered his voice to a whisper. "You are not a vampire. Neither of you are vampires."

"How... how do you know?" both girls talked at once.

"Because you've been holding that bunch of garlic flowers for the last several minutes and neither of you got ill."

"But..." Myrtle began.

"And another thing." Here he faltered. "Myrtle I..." He waited nervously and said nothing more. All the time he gazed into Myrtle's eyes.

It was getting dark and Felicity wanted to go home. "Please get it over with," she said. She went round to Freddy's back and gave him a shove, causing him to fall onto Myrtle, who instinctively grabbed him round the chest. Her glasses steamed up. Gently, Freddy took them off. "You are the most magical person I know," he said.

"I do like surds really," Myrtle said, and with that they kissed. Not a bite on the neck with two little dribbles of blood, but a proper kiss, a long kiss with lips.

Candice Goldman

Snow

I mostly know my neighbors by the clothes they hang on the dry cleaner
hangers in the front window of their flats—children's T-shirts, men and
women's underwear, dish towels.
It wasn't until "The Bachelor" TV program sprayed man-made snow down
our steep Russian Hill street—that many came out.
And this, after the "bachelor's" prospective girlfriends, on skis, in
bikinis—
had been filmed sliding down the hill and left.

White, clean, cold snow on a sunny spring day in May,
on Filbert Street in San Francisco.
Father comes out from waking up late after washing dishes or cooking up
Chow Fun or Mongolian Beef or Spicy Eggplant the night before.
Grandmother, hands tucked together, standing at the edge of the sidewalk
mystified, worried.

First daughter and second daughter bring her a snowball,
melting water dripping through their fingers.

I am there too with my granddaughter. She is 2 and to her this is no
stranger than the bus coming up the hill or the robin pecking at its
reflection in our dining room window.

At 67, I am the one enchanted and amazed.

Suzanne Patterson

Noise

In 2007, I lived on one of the noisiest streets, Avenida 5, in District Colonia del Norte, in one of the noisiest cities in the world, Mexico City. Landing on the sidewalks and streets of that crazy metropolis of cars, street vendors, truck vendors with megaphones, passing *pesaros* blaring music, honking chaos took my breath away. I fell in love with the City. The metro ran up and down Insurgentes Blvd, the longest street in Mexico City, and the traveling vendors with megaphones tuned up full blast—touted fruits, tamales, housewares, electronic devices, anything and everything loud!

Not only the streets—the sidewalks hummed with activity. Just beyond the door of my apartment—welcome to the largest black market in the world. On the sidewalks of Avenida 5 and every other business district in the city—the coveted and guarded spots passed on through generations touted restaurants with plastic tables and chairs, fresh juice bars, designer copies of everything imaginable including Gucci and Prada sunglasses, CDs and DVDs, jewelry, and makeup: There, 60% of the nation buys and sells goods without paying any taxes. It's referred to as the *Mercado Negrito* and there isn't a politician in all of Mexico who would touch it, because they would never win an election again.

People stand, talk, eat, laugh, socialize on the walkways at all times of night and day—you weave your way through them to go where you need to go. The people all seem to belong; to someone, to a family, to a church or a street-corner vendor.

Each workday I woke up, drank a coffee, ate a quick *quesadilla*, and left for the streets. A smiling woman fanned the charcoals of her little brassier on the corner, heating big pots of rice milk and chocolate for people passing by. We said *Buenos Dias,* and I sometimes bought a hot chocolate for the road.

The *Paseros*, small privately owned buses, cruised the numbered streets crossing the city between the subway and metro bus stations in the different districts. Usually driven by young, good-looking guys, they flaunted stereo systems that blasted salsas, hip-hop and mariachi music, all with good beats and strong bass. The cost—only three pesos.

Taxis blared their horns constantly, yelling *Va idiota*! and less polite phrases. For as sweet, happy and hospitable as Mexican people were, they became monsters behind the wheels of their cars. They honked and waved their fists at me even when I walked across pedestrian walkways with permitted lights. There were no silent periods in this city—none—ever.

Except—in the middle of the center of the noisiest city in the world—at the exact crosspoint of the X between Insurgentes Blvd and Reforma Ave—across from the Parque de Arte where artists exhibited their paintings every Sunday for fifty years, on a tiny street called Calle Rosa in District San Rafael, in my second apartment in Mexico City.

The apartment was actually part of a magnificent home built by President Perfidio Diaz, 100 years earlier for his daughter Christina in traditional Spanish style. The classy iron fence and gate opened by key onto a long courtyard. Shielded by French nineteenth-century street lamps and bordering flowering shrubs, each apartment had its own walkway and tiny porch before its door. The courtyard finished finely with a beautiful sculpture of a woman and a two-tiered fountain, which was turned on in the evening.

There were three levels to the building divided into 16 unique apartments, each possessing two or three levels. The second level had tiny black iron balconies that looked out over the courtyard. My apartment, number 16, was a loft apartment on the second floor at the back of the courtyard on the left. You entered through an open doorway by climbing a steep set of stairs to the second level. Number 16 was to the right.

Mexican Jonathan Beth

Upon first entering, you found yourself in a small intimate living room uniquely furnished with a simple couch, large wicker chair and comfortable and colorful floor pillows. Two eight-foot tall European-style windows on the left wall faced the courtyard. They opened out, and white chiffon curtains floated gently with the breezes blowing up the lane.

To the left of the windows was a gold banister circular stairway that scrolled its way up to the loft bedroom and bath. So charming—but wait! The ceiling, you must know about the ceiling; it was 20-feet high; Spanish red brick braceros-style arched trenches stretched across the ceiling. This was my dream apartment for an artist-in-residence in Mexico City—

But back to NOISE: This was the truly remarkable thing. Do you know when I shut the windows there was pure, uninterrupted silence in the room. *Realidad*! The walls of the apartment were 1½ feet thick. They buffered all sound. Oh! To die for. I was at home—home in the noisiest city of the world.

Clifford Hook

Riding with Pablo

Through miles of tangled jungle then crossing the tree line
Climbing up the rocky slope Why make this journey?
What drives him upward? Finally, exhausted, he arrives
Planetarium of the heart window to the other world
Leaping off place suddenly without warning, he
Jumps

Dancing dizzy among the stars spinning with the galaxies
Falling through space rising against the wind
Boundaries blasted coordinates crazily careening
Road of wandering stars spinning of the universe
Whisper of the Breath breathing of God
Waves of the cosmic ocean thunder on the beach
Swooping of eagles riding the rocket

Suddenly the stillness vast echoing emptiness
Floating drifting weightless dark cold bright intense
Glare of direct vision starry paths
Etched in your very heart branded with astral pathways
Searing immediacy racing past preparation
Rider falls from the horse it keeps racing the starry track
Becoming a bird a feather, a curved piece of ice
Racing racing then finally embodied
Standing again on this celestial platform

Playpen for the Soul university of higher learning
Infusion of star dust explosion of plodding mind
Limitless heart eaches out to the cosmos
Cosmos answers Yes Welcome my child

Wash yourself in the starry fountain
Stand before the throne The universe
Has been waiting for you

Clifford Hook

Hard Times

Plato missed	the funeral
What a mess	having your teacher executed
On some terrorist charge	which could be overturned later
But Socrates has	already left us
His date with eternity	could not be postponed
Plato is wary of Athens	he does a few
Book-signing tours	away from the City
Finally he leaves for Syracuse	living in a tyrant's court
Hoping to tame the beast	and somehow install his Republic
It is an old story	how an aging tyrant may toy with higher Ideas
While his young son	eager to make his mark
Will have no traffic	with Plato and his ideas
Plato returns to Athens	he wonders at the sacrifice
He looks over his shoulder	there is no one there

Jamirte Trott

Ceremonial Supper

Like a scene from a Renaissance painting
The table is oval, long and wide,
The tablecloth is of white linen.
The center adorned with bouquets
Of star-gazer lilies, yellow roses, peonies,
Interlaced with splashes of green leaves.

Around the table
Thirty people sit,
In countenance to the Friend
Who speaks of infinite love.

The stars shine above,
On a dark blue sky.

Set around the table,
Plates, forks, knifes,
Spoons,
Crystal wine glasses,
Candelabra.

Moonlight streams through the window.

Food doesn't matter much.
Water and wine
Symbols of life on earth
And in heaven.

Mirrors reflect the past
In between, quotations
From sages, saints, philosophers,
Politicians, poets, mathematicians.
Painters, poets, playwrights.

There are no cathedrals here,
No towers to make
The vision soar.
No cloister of buildings
To interrupt space
No traffic, no city lights
Yet it is here that past,
Present,
And future come together.

Prayer Brian Flynn

Adam and Eve Deborah McKay

Jamirte Trott

It is All Part of the Kingdom

I am the daughter of troubadours
Singing the news in public squares,
I speak to no one
I chant the news and leave.

What a structural gesture
By the hand of God
Man is.
So incomplete
So forlorn
He cannot see nor hear
Though before a tree he sees the fruit.

It is all part of the kingdom
The pine trees, the sky
The sun-dry palm tree
It is all part of prayer

He pleads with his eyes
He gives with his heart
Every now and then,
If at all

Through time he is bound
By the clock
Of the heavens he takes the rain
Through the earth he rides his horse.

He is not much more
Than a collection of desires.

It is all part of the kingdom,
It is all part of prayer.

Jamirte Trott

The Miraculous

To hear the voice
Of a god,
Speaking from the heavens
The pine trees stand
Tall and still,
Against the dome of the sky.
Cypress trees stand guard
All around the city.

The rivers are far away,
The oceans, the ports
The ships, the barges.
The vaporous powder-blue dome.
Bends over fields of flowers.

Bells toll above on the hill,
A mantel of green grass
Slopes down towards the city.
The deer reclines in the backyard,
His gaze towards infinity.
The hummingbirds return
Buzzing around the roses.
The clock clangs the hour
Suspended between heaven and earth.

Yosemite June Billings

Jamirte Trott

Island

It is three o'clock in the afternoon
The history of man goes on.
It is Sunday,
The atmosphere is hazy.

The weather, the beach, the island,
The bridge…
Contrast with
The crowd that dresses as if
For a New Year's Eve ball.
They are the many
Who came to the beach
On a Sunday afternoon
To stand still,
As an Egyptian sculpture.

She wears seven to nine petticoats
Her husband in his suit
Occupies much less space than her
She holds the leash of time,
The black dog tied to the other end.

Some are here to enjoy,
As the girl who plays hula hoop,
The black dog that sniffs the sand,
The man in sleeveless T-shirt
Who reclines on his elbow
And gazes at the water.
Everyone else just stands,
They are the many
Who came to the beach
On a Sunday afternoon
To stand still,
As an Egyptian sculpture.

On a Sunday afternoon
At the Island of the Grand Jatte.

Ascending Yanna Bat-Adam

Jamirte Trott

Epitaph

From the abundant generosity
Of the earth,
I take the pristine, blue sky
Of spring, and early fall,
From there I take as well,
The vastness of the ocean.
From the animal world,
I take the dog, the cat, the tiger.
From the complications of humanity
I take my love for you, my Beloved.

www.ingramcontent.com/pod-product-compliance
Lightning Source LLC
Chambersburg PA
CBHW040821050726
47507CB00021B/95
9780692484814